Series Editor: Sue Hewer

3

WWW The Internet

Terry Atkinson

The views expressed in this publication are the author's and do not necessarily represent those of CILT.

Acknowledgements

I wish to acknowledge the work of Oliver Rowland, whose guide to the Internet, an unpublished PGCE assignment, provided some of the ideas used in this book. Help and inspiration was also drawn from colleagues on the MFLIT steering group and especially Pam Haezewindt. The work of teachers in various schools was used in some of the case studies. Special thanks are due to languages teachers and their students in Priory School, North Somerset, Nailsea School, North Somerset and Clifton College, Bristol. Thanks are also due to David Wilson, some of whose ideas were used to illustrate activities, and to Sue Hewer for her advice and support.

Finally, I wish to thank Lucy Atkinson, for her support, encouragement and many practical suggestions and comments.

First published in 1998

ISBN 1 874016 90 9

A catalogue record for this book is available from the British Library
Printed in Great Britain by Copyprint UK Ltd
Cover design and photography: Marc Padellec

Published by the Centre for Information on Language Teaching and Research, 20 Bedfordbury, Covent Garden, London WC2N 4LB

CILT Publications are available from: Grantham Book Services, Isaac Newton Way, Alma Park Industrial Estate, Grantham, Lincs NG31 8SD. Tel: 01476 541 080. Fax: 01476 541 061. Book trade representation (UK and Ireland): Broadcast Book Services, 24 De Montfort Road, London SW16 1LZ. Tel: 0181 677 5129.

Contents

1 What is the Internet?

The Internet provides a window on the world that can bring foreign languages and culture into the classroom. It is a dynamic, authentic resource that can enrich language learning in many new and exciting ways. Exploiting this resource is a challenge for languages teachers and this book is designed to provide guidance in adapting to the medium.

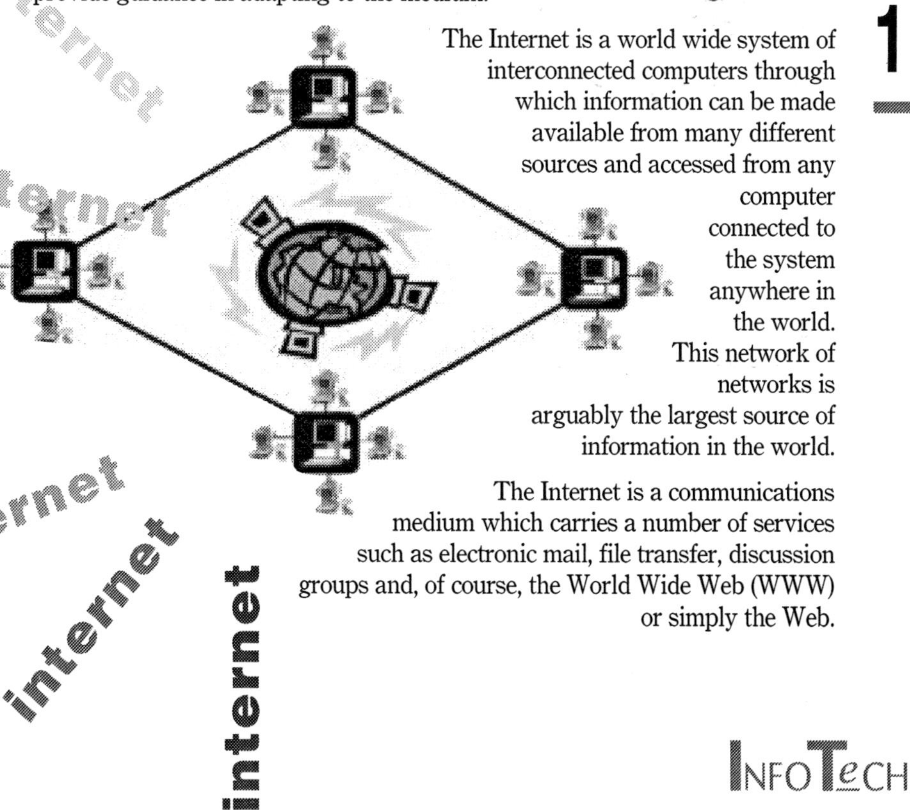

The Internet is a world wide system of interconnected computers through which information can be made available from many different sources and accessed from any computer connected to the system anywhere in the world. This network of networks is arguably the largest source of information in the world.

The Internet is a communications medium which carries a number of services such as electronic mail, file transfer, discussion groups and, of course, the World Wide Web (WWW) or simply the Web.

Electronic mail (e-mail)

E-mail is usually text based and messages are sent and may be read sooner, later or not at all, just as with conventional mail (asynchronous). Live e-mail is also possible with the screen splitting to show outgoing and incoming messages (synchronous). E-mail can be used to send data such as documents, picture files, audio files or computer programs as attachments to messages. See InfoTech 1, *E-mail* by Kate Townshend, for details of using e-mail in language learning.

Discussion groups

There are discussion groups in many languages and on every conceivable topic. Some discussion groups are live (IRC) and some are asynchronous (e.g. Usenet). Many discussion groups deal with unsavoury or unsuitable topics so that any use would best be restricted to adult learners unless younger users are very carefully supervised. The following examples show the kind of messages that are sent to chat groups and include the bizarre, the obnoxious and an awful lot of authentic but inaccurate language.

Statut: Date:22/12/97 De:Valentin

Bien le bonjour à toutes ces dames... (...pis les gars aussi mais en moins "doux")

Je voulais seulement vous souhaiter à TOUS, de très Joyeuses Fêtes...

Que 98 vous apporte joie, bonheur, santé... et fun sur le chat... Si tout le monde y met un peu du sien et utilise ce "passe-temps" intelligemment, ca demeurera un "jeu" agréable et utile aussi pour plusieurs d'en nous qui y trouve amis et confidents... ...et y mettre un peu du sien, ce n'est pas seulement avec les autres utilisateurs mais çà veut aussi dire avec vos conjoints et conjointes respectif et RESPCTABLE. Faites les pas "chier" avec votre habitude... ...La modération a bien meilleurs goût... :) En parlant de ça, ben amusez vous bien pis prennez un coup solide si çà vous tente... mais prenez Nez Rouge ou ben embarquez avec un copain (si yé pas aussi faite que vous). on vous aime... vivant... (coudon yé ben moralisateur lui tout d'un coup....mais c'est comme ça)

Encore une fois....Bonne et heureuse année 98...

Valentin

Date:23/12/97
De:Sangoku

Salut gang!
queque chose m'échappe:
puisque je suis nouveau, ça
parrait ordinaire mais,
comment on fait pour
chatter? aussi, mon nom
n'est pas affiché sur la liste
des membres et j'en suis un!
Aidez moi s.v.p.!

le nouveau dit: Sangoku____

Statut:
Date:24/12/97
De:Geneviève

Bonjour à tous les europeens,

Je suis Quebecoise et j'aimerais
pouvoir chater avec vous "les
europeens
qui biensur parlent français"
Ecrivez moi sur mon e-mail que voici
: larocque@ ntic.qc.ca
ça me ferais plaisir de vous
répondre!!!

J'en profite pour vous souhaiter un
JOYEUX NOËL ET BONNE ANNEE
et faite attention à vous....
Geneviève
XXX

Statut:

Date:22/12/97

De:Les bananes en pyjamas

Nous sommes 2 Québécoises et
nous voulons parler avec quelqu'un!

On se nomme "Les bananes en
pyjamas".On attend de vos
nouvelles!

File transfer

There are FTP (file transfer protocol) sites which are, essentially, catalogues of software and other data that can be downloaded via the Internet. All types of software are available — commercial, educational, games, business. Much of the software is free or free for a trial period. This software is sometimes termed **freeware** (no charge) or **shareware** – you can download and use for a trial period but have to pay to use the software fully. Data files could include documents such as syllabuses, worksheets, exam papers, etc. OFSTED[1] reports can be downloaded in this way and it is likely that the Internet will gradually become the main medium for publishing documents to schools and colleges, as proposed in the National Grid for Learning (NGFL) consultation document. Downloaded OFSTED reports are in the form of a word processed document that can be loaded into the word processor and printed or read on screen.

Downloading language learning software may also be of interest to teachers. There are some language programs available from sites in other countries, for example the Centre National De Documentation Pédagogique[2] in France has an interesting word puzzle called *Le jeu du Mai* which can be downloaded as a working demonstration. This and other sites are just being established so there is not much material available yet. Another working demonstration of software that can be downloaded from Lingu@NET[3] is Camsoft's *Fun With Texts.*

The World Wide Web

The focus of this book is the World Wide Web which is the key information resource on the Internet. Information on the Web may be in the form of text, pictures, video or sound or, increasingly, multi-media. The illustration opposite is a typical Web page for a newspaper.

1 http://www.open.gov.uk/ofsted/ofsted.htm
2 http://www.cndp.fr/
3 http://www.becta.org.uk/projects/linguanet/index.html

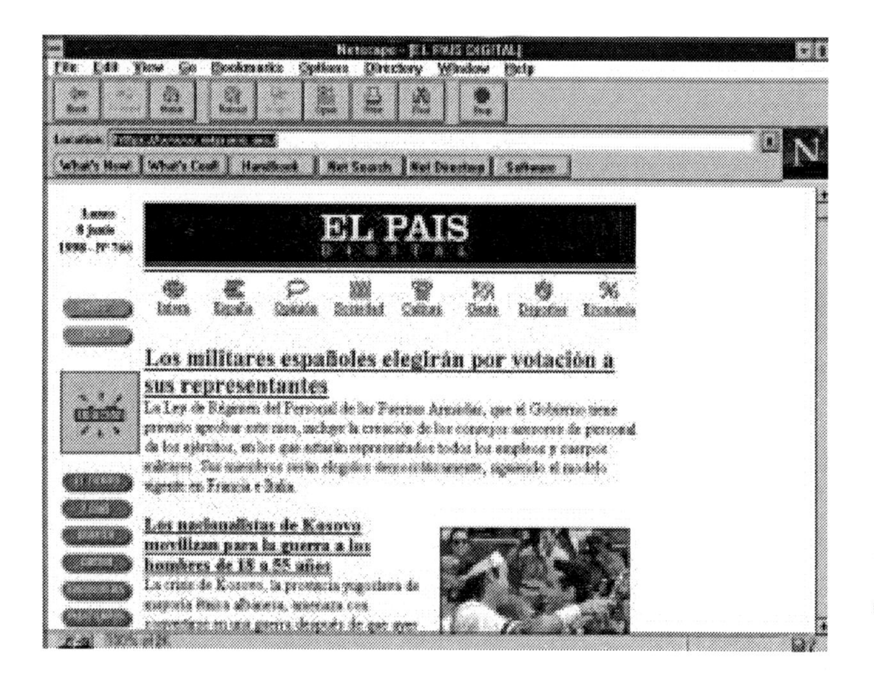

These pages of information for the Web are usually stored on powerful computer systems or servers which can be accessed readily from any modern computer via a modem and a telephone line. The Web is the main format for providing information which is displayed as text and images on screen and which usually has links to other Web sites of relevance. The link can be to another place on the same page or on the same Web site but can also be to a different Web site located anywhere in the world. Linking is a very powerful feature. Any text or image can be used as a link. If a word or phrase links to another place on the Web, it usually appears in a different colour to the rest of the text and/or it is underlined. The user can then choose to follow the link or ignore it. To follow the link involves moving the mouse pointer to the link word and clicking. The new page will then be downloaded and the old page is replaced. Some of these features are illustrated in the screen shot on the next page, taken from Netscape 3.

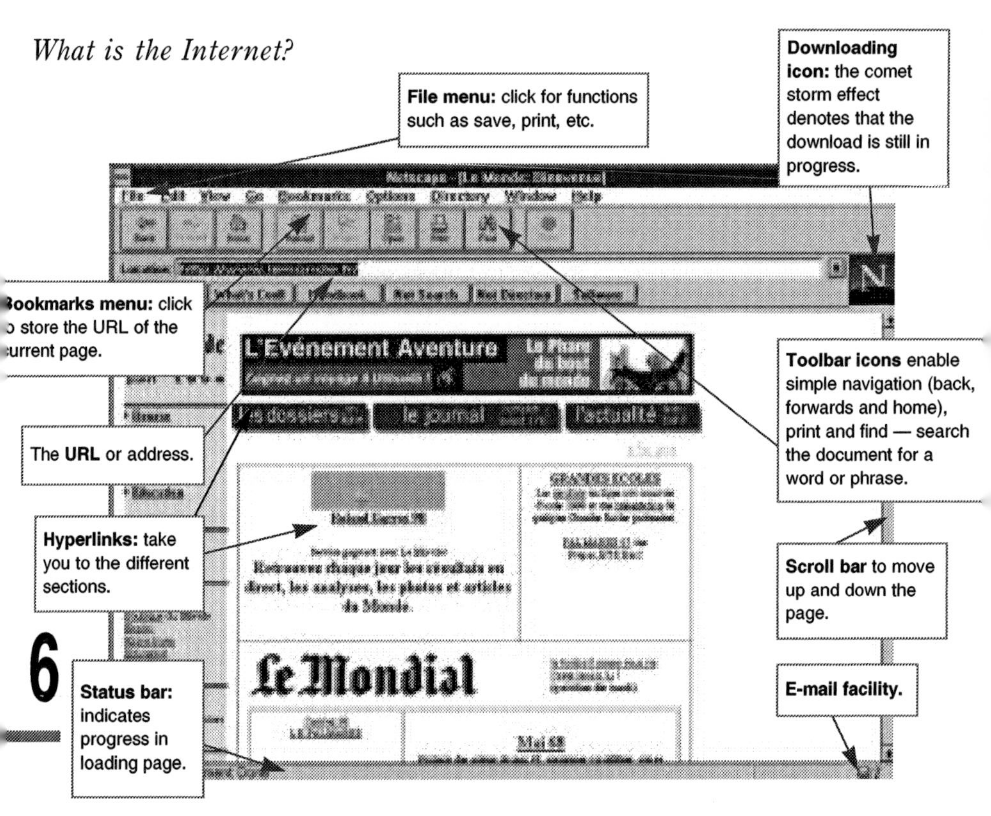

THE INTERNET AND LANGUAGE LEARNING

The Internet, and especially the WWW, is the largest and most accessible collection of authentic resources available to teachers. It is constantly growing and is continually being updated, allowing an immediacy not previously possible. These resources are in electronic form which allows for flexible use on the computer on a range of applications — word processor, text manipulation, multi-media authoring. Equally, the information can be printed onto paper or, in the case of sound, recorded onto tape.

As well as the advantages of quantity, quality, diversity and flexibility these materials offer the same opportunities and the same problems as other authentic materials. They bring with them authentic language, for example the language of youth cultures. One of the principle benefits of using authentic materials is this cultural authenticity and Web pages are particularly useful with regard to the latest trends, be these in fashion, language, art or whatever.

There are sites of strong local, regional or national character so that diversity of culture is reflected. The cultural element is one of the key benefits of any authentic resource, but the exploitation of the materials is dependent upon the skills of the teacher since these materials are not produced specifically for learning activities.

As well as authentic material the WWW also has a lot of useful information for the languages teacher on such matters as teaching and learning methods, using IT in language learning, professional development opportunities, software for language learning, guides to finding resources on the Internet, OFSTED reports, catalogues of teaching and learning materials, including some which can be freely downloaded, and much more.

There are also a number of sites that offer services to language learners and users, such as machine translation, on-line dictionaries, virtual language schools, on-line language activities, links and exchanges.

Publishing on the Internet is another interesting possibility. Most schools now have their own site and an increasing number publish students' work via this medium. A particular advantage for languages is that students' work in the foreign language can be read by native speakers and other speakers/learners of the language. It may be possible to obtain feedback on students' work, although this will probably only happen if the audience is clearly targeted, e.g. a link school.

The Web is invaluable for access to up-to-date material in the lesser taught languages. There are many Web sites in major languages such as Chinese, Russian, Japanese, Urdu, Spanish, Portuguese, Italian, etc. The display of different character sets for the various languages requires the browser software to be configured appropriately. Some Web sites provide guides to interesting sites in many different languages:

WWW Foreign Languages Resources
http://www.itp.berkeley.edu/~thorne/HumanResources.html

World Language Pages
http://www.livjm.ac.uk/language

Web Sites for Languages
http://www.becta.org.uk/projects/ linguanet/websites/index.html

Information providers on the World Wide Web

Anyone can become an information provider on the Web. Many large companies have Web sites, especially those in the communications industries. There is a significant educational presence on the Web of schools and colleges. Universities have used the Internet for a number of years so that some have developed sophisticated systems ushering in the age of the virtual university.

However, there are also many small voluntary organisations and individuals who have sites. It is these sites which give the Internet character and diversity, making it a unique medium enabling many to communicate with many.

The range of information available can be seen from the list of categories offered on Yahoo's French page:

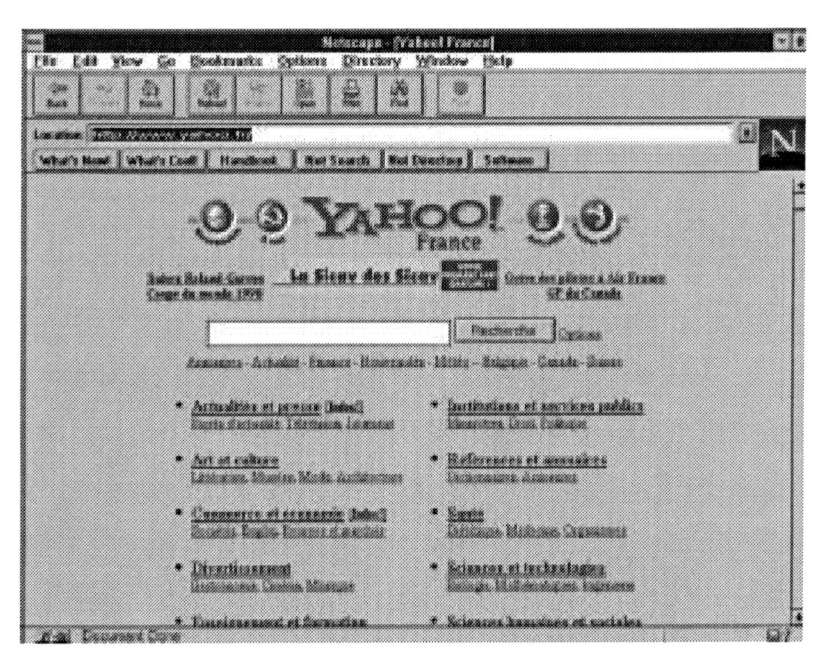

Each of these categories leads on to sub-categories and to listings of dozens of sites within each sub-category, for example, at the time of writing *Gastronomie* lead on to the following sub-categories:

Category	Number of sites
Aliments	18
Boissons	100+
Emploi	1
Evénements	2
Fromages	16
Jeux avec la nourriture	100+
Recettes	23
Restaurants	82
Sociétés	100+
Végétarisme	4

In addition, nineteen sites were listed under the main heading of *Gastronomie*. Each of these has a hyperlink which allows you to go directly to the site, and for most there is also a brief description of what the site is about. These are shown below as an example of what might be available but the actual links are not given because many will change during the lifetime of this publication. However, many others will continue to be available via Yahoo France[4] and other search engines.

Association Saveurs de Provence.

Association d'étudiants en Maîtrise de LEA à l'Université d'Avignon ayant pour objet de promouvoir les produits agro-alimentaires et viticoles provençaux.

Bernatchez, Eric — Boycott : fait de vous un consommateur non seulement averti mais engagé.

Confrérie des Gastronomes Picards — Groupe de spécialistes de la gastronomie, de l'hôtellerie et de la restauration.

Cuisine lyonnaise avec Paul Bocuse, La — Spécialités, quelques recettes, histoire et les grandes tables.

French baker's club — Rassemble les professionnels de la boulangerie et la pâtisserie artisanales pour organiser un échange de savoir-faire sur le plan international.

Gastronomie du Cantal — Produits de la ferme, marchés du pays, étapes gourmandes et fromages du Cantal.

Gastronomie en Haute Savoie — Fondue et raclette sont les plus connues, mais d'autres spécialités sont tout aussi savoureuses et méritent d'être goûtées.

Gastronomie en Périgord — Art culinaire, conserves et produits gastronomiques.

Gastronomie européenne — Conseils pratiques, cuisine, vins et événements.

Goudots Gourmand Aurillac, Les — Manifestation gastronomique. Les consommateurs sont invités à gouter et à juger les différents produits régionaux.

Guylian — Historique et produits.

Historique de la Poutine — Tout l'histoire de la création de la fameuse et juteuse poutine.

Liebig Maille Amora.

Miel, Le — Le miel et ses bienfaits.

Reuille, Stéphane — Un pâtissier propose aux gourmands de faire découvrir son métier et ses recettes.

Saveurs du Monde — Encyclopédies culinaires, recettes et répertoire des restaurants.

Web Cuisine — La cuisine française, étrangère et des recettes.

fr.rec.cuisine — Groupe de discussion non modéré consacré à la gastronomie, aux arts culinaires et à l'échange de recettes.

4 http://www.yahoo.fr/

GETTING ON-LINE

As with any other aspect of IT usage in school, liaison with the IT co-ordinator/manager is vital. He or she will have the solution to many of your technical questions. A book such as this can offer only general advice whereas the IT teacher in school can advise on the specifics of your context, the hardware and software that is available in your school and the type of Internet connection that is available. Moreover, the IT co-ordinator has an overview of the IT skills and needs of students across the curriculum.

Schools and colleges have rapidly acquired Internet connections and there should be access, albeit limited, for most languages teachers. For those without ready access at school it may be possible to arrange access at a local teachers' centre or at CILT or one of the regional network of Comenius centres. Public access to the Internet is now available in libraries and other outlets.

Increasingly, teachers may consider home use of the Internet, but whether for home or school use the basic requirements are the same:

The computer

While almost any computer can be used, the Internet places particular demands upon the system which calls for a high specification. A modern, fast, multi-media system with a large hard disk and lots of RAM will allow information to be accessed quickly, reducing on-line costs, and will also allow maximum exploitation of the facilities provided by the Internet.

Fortunately, the Internet is not tied to any particular type of computer so that all makes can be connected — PC, Apple Macintosh or Acorn. Compatibility is one of the key assets of the Internet.

The telephone

A telephone line is needed to connect to the Internet and any line will do. Heavy use would require a dedicated line but it is perfectly possible to switch between Internet use and normal telephone or fax. At the time of writing, faster information flow can be achieved with an ISDN line. This would be useful if large amounts of data are to be transferred, e.g. video.

The modem

A modem is needed to connect the computer to the telephone line. Some computers have a built-in modem and others can be fitted with an internal modem, but external modems are also common. Modems are developing rapidly with new, faster standards being introduced annually. The speed of the modem is one of the factors determining the speed at which you can access information. However, a high speed modem may not be worth the expense if your computer or phone line are not capable of operating at high speeds.

The Internet service

In reality there are usually two services provided:

- connection to the Internet with e-mail address;
- information services.

There are a large number of Internet service providers who will enable you to connect to their host computer and thence to the Internet. Service providers offer a range of services reflected in differing price scales. The most basic service offers an e-mail address and access to the Internet through a telephone number local to you. More advanced facilities would include multiple e-mail addresses and Web space for you to publish your own pages. Some providers offer extensive information, news and entertainment services as well as help with accessing the WWW and, in some cases, screening of undesirable material. Usually, the subscription charge includes the cost of the browser software (see below) needed to access the Web and covers future software upgrades. For those contemplating a subscription from home it is worth checking that you will be getting the browser you are familiar with at school. Some service providers, for example Research Machines and British Telecom, have specialised in the educational sector and offer facilities designed especially for schools and colleges, including curriculum support.

The software

To view WWW pages on your computer screen you will require a browser. This software converts the data received via your phone line to text and images. As with most software, there are a range of browsers available and new ones or new versions of old ones appear at regular intervals. At the time of writing the most

common browsers in use are Netscape and Microsoft Internet Explorer. There is little to choose between them so, as with all generic software, it is best to use whichever one is most readily available and used by students in other curricular areas. It is worth noting that target language versions of browsers are available and can be downloaded from the Internet sites of the software companies – Microsoft[5] and Netscape[6]. Using a target language browser enhances language learning by immersing the student in the language and providing the opportunity for purposeful language use. Here is a screen shot of the French version of Internet Explorer:

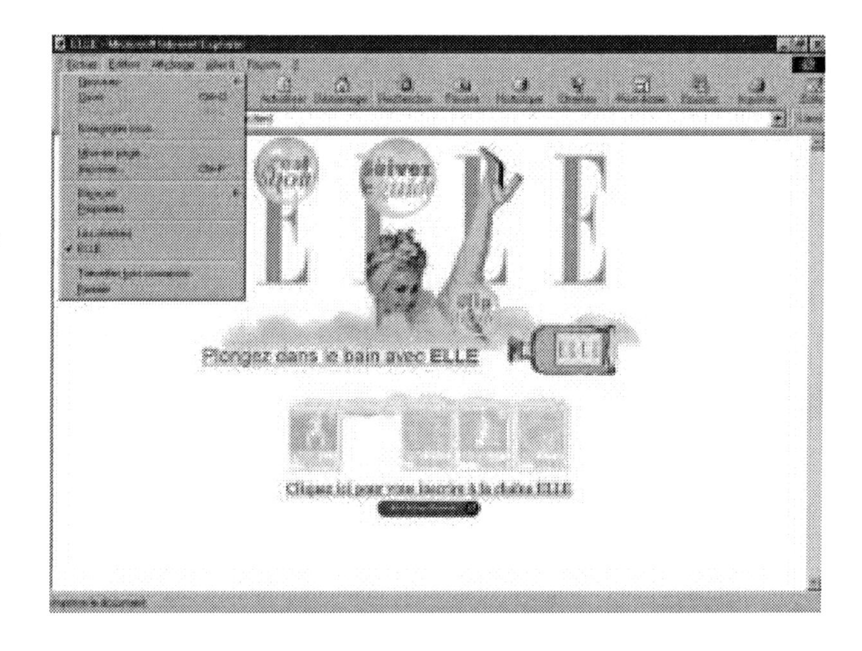

5 http://microsoft.com/ie_intl/fr/
6 http://home.netscape.com/fr/
For both URLs, you can change fr to it (Italy), de (Germany) or es (Spain).

Costs

Two types of cost need to be budgeted for. Firstly, the initial cost of the computer equipment — computer system, modem, printer (a printer is useful to print out materials for use in class) and software. Secondly, there are recurrent costs for the telephone line rental, the call charges (usually local rate call charges apply), monthly subscription to your service provider and, in some cases, on-line charges. Some service providers charge for time on-line above a certain limit while others offer free unlimited time on line. Thereafter, the Internet is largely a free service. At present, for example, most major newspapers around the world can be accessed free of charge. It may be that in the future a charge will be made or that the costs will be born through advertising. Hyperlinks can take you straight from the pages of a newspaper to the catalogue of a retailer where you can shop on-line. Whatever happens, there will continue to be much on the Internet that will be free.

Dangers

Offensive material does exist on the Internet for those determined to find it. It is possible to come across such material inadvertently, as did an Internet user quoted in a Which? magazine article who, in searching for information on the X files, came across X-rated sites. Various steps can be taken to limit this danger:

- subscribe to an Internet service that screens out offensive material;
- closely supervise on-line use of the Internet;
- use the Internet off-line, perhaps by developing an Intranet;
- restrict open access to the Internet for younger students;
- provide access for older students in libraries, where some supervision may be possible;
- require users to contract into a code of conduct.

The status and accuracy of material found on the Internet is another cause for concern. It should be remembered that anyone can put up anything so that students need to develop the skill of assessing the validity of information through verification of sources.

Close monitoring of student usage will be needed to avoid excessive costs being incurred. For example, reading a long text in the TL on-line may take some time and can be accomplished as readily off-line.

Copyright issues with regard to the Internet are unclear. Materials can be downloaded or printed out readily. In fact, this will be what many languages teachers will want to do. Much of the material is not protected so that copyright is not an issue. For other materials, it is fair to adopt the same policy as for printed matter, i.e. that educational use within your own school or college of a proportion (10%) of the material is acceptable whereas wholesale usage or commercial exploitation is not. In many cases WWW sites list contact addresses (usually e-mail) so that permissions can be sought. In some cases Web pages do reserve copyright, but many do not.

Surfing the Internet is an image that has some accuracy and relevance. There is a temptation to jump from link to link, taking in the superficial aspects of each page and not reading or absorbing the material. If used on-line in this way, the Internet may lead to limited learning. Detailed study may be better encouraged by printing out pages or by saving them to disk for off-line access.

Much of the material on the Internet is in English. In addition, some sites offer English language versions as well as the language of origin. It has been estimated that 5% of the WWW is in French and this represents a considerable amount of material. The danger remains that students may spend too much time looking at material in English. This is another reason why it may be better for teachers to pre-select material to be printed or saved to disk for off-line access.

Perhaps the most frustrating aspect of the WWW is the time it can take to download information. Even on an ultra-fast modern computer a page may take several minutes to arrive and, on occasions, may not appear at all. This is caused by congestion of the Internet which can become as grid locked as the motorways on a bank holiday weekend. Congestion tends to be at its worst in the afternoon and evenings as users in North America come on-line. Thus, an afternoon lesson on-line may be unproductive.

Summary

The World Wide Web provides an invaluable resource for language learning. The task ahead is to ensure that languages teachers have ready access to this new medium which has a very special value for language learning in particular. How to exploit this resource is a key issue and a whole new methodology is being developed which will be explored further through the subsequent chapters of this book.

2 Searching the Web

There is a vast amount of information on the Web so that there is a need for skills and tools that enable successful searches to be made. Finding material on the Internet is possible in various ways. There are special software tools, known as search engines, which enable you to search for information. The other main way of finding sites is by following links from one WWW page to another — some sites contain a Web guide to a specific topic and contain lists of links. There are a number of such pages for different language-related topics. Web searching skills are important as they will enable you to find just what you are looking for rather than relying on sites recommended in this book or elsewhere. Students also need to learn how to search the Web if they are to carry out research activities.

NAVIGATING THE WEB

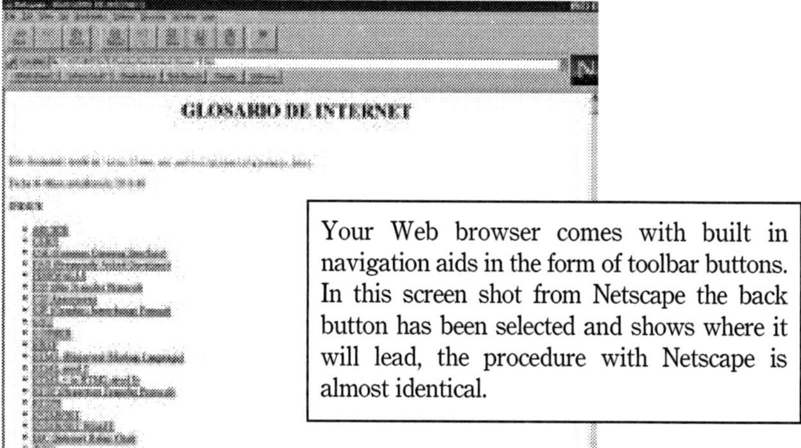

Your Web browser comes with built in navigation aids in the form of toolbar buttons. In this screen shot from Netscape the back button has been selected and shows where it will lead, the procedure with Netscape is almost identical.

Use of these buttons will allow you to return to a page that you have looked at previously (BACK button) and then move forward again to the most recently visited site (FORWARD button). The GO menu contains a list of the last few sites visited so that you can jump to any of them. The HOME button takes you to your home page – this can be set to any page and is usually set to the institutional home page or that of your Internet service provider.

Some Web sites have navigation aids for the site. A common system is the use of frames to have part of the page partitioned, giving a list of the main contents of the site in the form of links, so that you can instantly move from any part of the site to any other.

SEARCH ENGINES

There are a number of freely available search engines on the Internet that can find sites that match your criteria in a few seconds. Search engines can be global in character, aiming to find anything on the WWW, or more specific to a topic or country. Search engines may be language specific but many are truly multi-lingual, able to operate in many different languages and to search for information in all languages or in the language of your choice.

One of the best known and fastest global search engines is Altavista (http://altavista.digital.com) which operates in a range of languages and from sites in different countries. Its main rival is Yahoo! which, in addition to its main global search, is also developing country specific facilities, among them France and Germany. There are other search engines which operate at a national or mono-lingual level and sites containing useful links. Relevant URLs are listed below. As indicated earlier, URLs do change. You should always check out in advance any URL you plan to use in class.

French

Yahoo France	http://www.yahoo.fr
Ecila	http://www.ecila.ceic.com/
Lokace	http://www.lokace.com/
infoseek France	http://www.infoseek.com/Home?pg=Home.html&sv=FR
francite	http://www.francite.com
carrefour	http://www.carrefour.net/
UREC	http://www.urec.fr/France

Echo	http://echo.fr/
Nomade	http://www.nomade.fr/
Tout en un	http://195.6.175.197:80/provider/resource/allinone
Sam Acorus' guide	http://sam.acorus.fr/referenceur/liste_franco.htm
Swiss search	http://www.search.ch/
Swiss Web	http://swiss.Web.ch/

German

Yahoo	http://www.yahoo.de
Aladin	http://www.aladin.de/neuerl.html
Crawler	http://www.crawler.de/
Eule	http://www.eule.de/addurl.html
Excite Germany	http://www.excite.de/info/add_url.html
Hotlist Germany	http://www.hotlist.de/neueintrag.html
Intersearch Germany	http://germany.intersearch.net/add.html
Lycos Germany	http://www.lycos.de/
Neuzugang	http://www.web-archiv.de/index.html
Swiss search	http://www.search.ch/
Swiss Web	http://swiss.web.ch/
Fux	http://www.fux.de/

Spanish

Ole	http://www.ole.es/
Red iris	http://www.rediris.es/
Directorio (Latin America/ Spain)	http://www.virtualizar.com/buscar/
La Brujula (Argentina)	http://www.brujula.com.ar/
Auyantepui (Venezuela)	http://www.auyantepui.com/
El indice	http://www.ELINDICE.COM

Italian

Arianna	http://www.arianna.it/
multisoft	http://search/multisoft.it/
Swiss search	http://www.search.ch/
Swiss Web	http:/swiss/web.ch/
Cerca	http://www.cercainternet.it/

Panjabi

Languages of the Indian sub-continent	http://www.hull.ac.uk/cti/langsite/indian.htm
Prasad Naik's India Links	http://www.ee.ualberta.ca/~naik/india.html
Community languages	http:www.becta.org.uk/projects/linguanet/websites/britain.html#Community

Using a search engine (some examples)

Altavista Spanish

Here is an example of a search using Altavista to find the Spanish newspaper, *El Pais.*

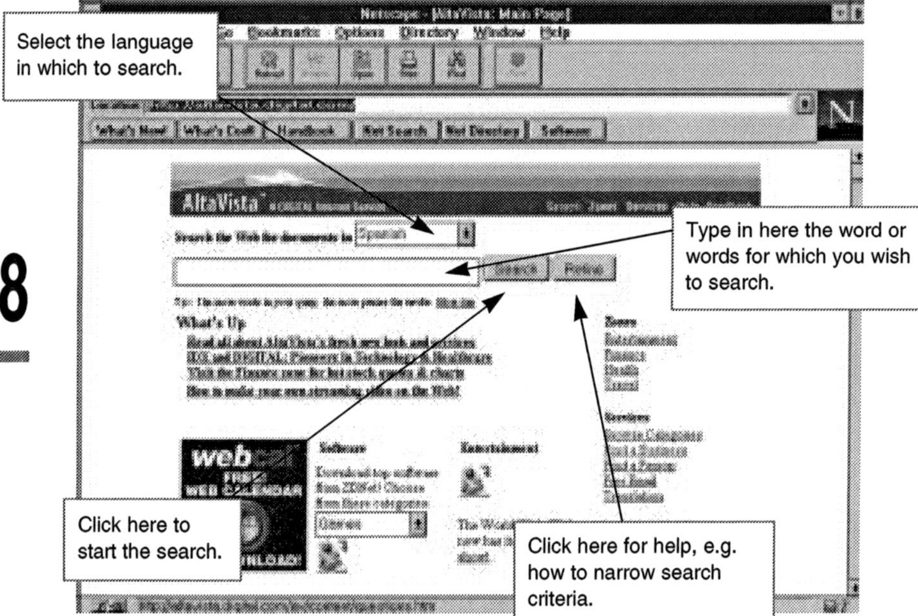

Note the use of speech marks which ensures that only sites containing both words will be found. If speech marks are not used, sites with either word will be found, resulting in many unwanted hits. More advanced search criteria are given on the Altavista help page.

A word search using Yahoo! France

Type Camembert in the box and then press the enter key to begin the 'recherche'.

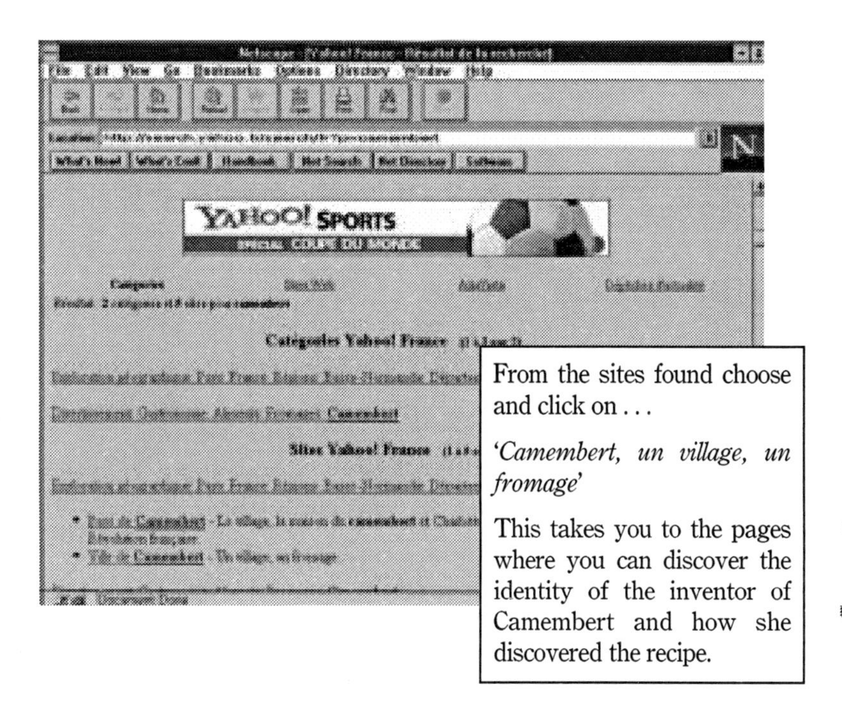

A category search using Yahoo! France

Use the Yahoo! France search engine[7] to conduct a hierarchical search. For example, select each category and sub-category as follows:

Divertissements >>>> Bande dessinée et animation >>>> BD >>>> titres

Among the various titles listed you will find Astérix with a number of sites listed, including the official site.[8]

7 http://www.yahoo.fr/
8 http://www.asterix.tm.fr/

WEB GUIDES

A Web guide is a page or pages on the WWW containing a guide to sites of relevance to a specific topic. There are specific Web guides for languages, language teaching and language learning:

ALL	http://www.bris.ac.uk/Depts/Education/all.htm
BBC	http://www.bbc.co.uk/education/languages/
CILT	http://www.cilt.org.uk
CTI Centre for Modern Languages at the University of Hull	http://www.hull.ac.uk/cti/
Human languages page	http://www.june29.com/HLP/
Lingu@NET: a virtual language centre	http://www.becta.org.uk/projects/linguanet/index.html (check)
Schools On Line	http://sol.ultralab.anglia.ac.uk/pages/schools_online/languages/mflhome.html
Teaching with the Web	http://polyglot.lss.wisc.edu/lss/lang/teach.html
World Language Pages	http://www.livjm.ac.uk/language
WWW Foreign Languages Resources	http://www.itp.berkeley.edu/~thorne/HumanResources.html
Bristol University Language Centre	http://www.bris.ac.uk/Depts/LangCent/French/resourc1.htm

There are also Web guides in the various languages for a range of topic areas, for example *le cinéma* in France.

INTERNET MAGAZINES

These so-called e-zines offer a more serendipitous selection of material and there are a growing number in the various languages such as:

French

Frogmag	http://www.princeton.edu/~tobypaff/frogmag/home.html
Label France	http://www.france.diplomatie.fr/label_france/
France Com	http://www.france.com/mag/index.html
Le Magazine de l'An 2000	http://www.francetelecom.fr/bin/page.cgi/vfrance/magazine/maganv3.htm
Planète Internet	http://www.club-internet.fr/planete/

German

Digital mirror — http://www.digitalmirror.de/
Zongo — http://www.nineties.com/zongo/zongo4.html
biwidus — http://biwidus.ch/

Italian

Over forty electronic publications are listed here — http://www.arianna.it/arianna/catalog/Informazione_e_Notizie/Pubblicazioni_Elettroniche.html

Spanish

Kong — http://www.iponet.es/kong/index.htm
Matices (in German!) — http://www.is-koeln.de/matices/

BOOKMARKING/FAVOURITE SITES

Finding sites can take time, so it is useful to be able to mark a site so that you can go directly to it. In Netscape this is known as bookmarking and is a powerful feature which can be operated quite easily. To bookmark a site you first need to go to the site. Once the site has been loaded and you have on screen the particular page you want to bookmark, you need to click on the bookmark menu at the top of the screen and then click 'Add bookmark'.

The site will now be added to the list on the bookmark menu and can be found again very quickly, simply by clicking on the bookmark menu and then on the site reference that will now appear there.

If you are using Microsoft's Internet Explorer, the procedure is known as Favourite Sites but works in the same way. If you use the WWW regularly, you will soon accumulate lots of bookmarks. These can be organised into different groups by using folders. You can also save bookmarks onto a floppy disk — useful if you want to give access to a class.

Hints on searching the Internet

1. Switch off autoload graphics for faster searching — you can switch on when you have found the site you are looking for.

2. URLs can tell you something about the source of the information:. The final two letters represent the country of origin, e.g. fr = France, uk = United Kingdom, de = Germany, es = Spain. Where no country code is given, the address is usually from the USA.

3. Immediately before the country code is another code which indicates the nature of the organisation, e.g. gov/gouv – government, ac – academic, co — commercial organisation or company, org: -non-profit-making organisation, ~ private individual. In the USA, URLs are different with no country marker and with different organisational codes, e.g. edu — educational, com – commercial. Some non US companies have also managed to obtain .com addresses so the country code is not then used.

4. You need to type in URLs correctly to the last digit. One mistake will invalidate the URL and lead to an error message.

5. If you place the mouse pointer over a link, the following will happen:
   1 the URL appears at the bottom of the screen;
   2 left mouse button click will take you to the link;
   3 right mouse click brings up a menu of various items including facility to copy the URL (e.g. for entry into your bookmark file).

6. Opening a **location** if you know the URL or Internet address:
   1 click on the File menu;
   2 click on Open or Open Location;
   3 type in the address;
   4 press return.

   If this doesn't work, check that the address has been typed correctly.

7. If you find a page of links and wish to explore the links one by one, you can avoid having to re-load the page of links by opening a new browser — have the link page in the old browser, copy the link you want and go to it in the new browser (not recommended for machines with limited memory or slow speed of operation).

8. Sometimes sites are down or malfunctioning, so you will not be able to access them until or unless they are repaired. Even when the site is in place, it may be congested so that you cannot access it. This is akin to an engaged telephone line.

9. You can search for a word or phrase on a Web page by using Find. Either click on the toolbar icon or select Find from the Edit menu.

10. A good way to search for sites relating to a specific aspect of the language is to type in a word or phrase, for example, *je me lève* — to find sites relating to daily routine

11. To search for images, type in the subject with the file extension .gif or .jpg (these are the main image formats used on the WWW). In one search — "chateau.gif" — over 700 images were found using Yahoo France, including the one shown on the right.

Summary

The Web makes the world of the foreign language accessible via your computer and there are a range of techniques and skills that can help you to explore this exciting opportunity. However, from one or two simple sites you will soon discover many more. For a quick start make sure that you can:

- use the navigation buttons on your Web browser;
- log on and explore Lingu@NET or any other virtual languages centre;
- find sites of interest via Yahoo France or Yahoo Germany or the appropriate search engine/Web guide for the language(s) you are interested in;
- bookmark sites that you wish to re-visit.

3 Using the Net for language learning

The Web provides an abundance of authentic materials that can be used in many different ways. The exploitation of authentic materials is well documented[9] and many familiar ideas can be used with this new medium. Material can be printed out, used on line or off line or in other IT applications such as word processing.

Using printouts of Web pages

A simple way to get started is to print out pages from the Web and photocopy these for use with a class. This works best with simple Web sites where the Web page will print onto one or two sides of A4. Here are some examples:

Canadian weather map

The weather map can be used to support oral or written work with the usual range of questions. Note that the dating of the map enables the use of tenses, including the future tense, if you download a map of tomorrow's outlook.

9 For example, Little D, S Devitt and D Singleton, *Learning foreign languages from authentic texts: theory and practice* (Dublin: Authentik, 1989)

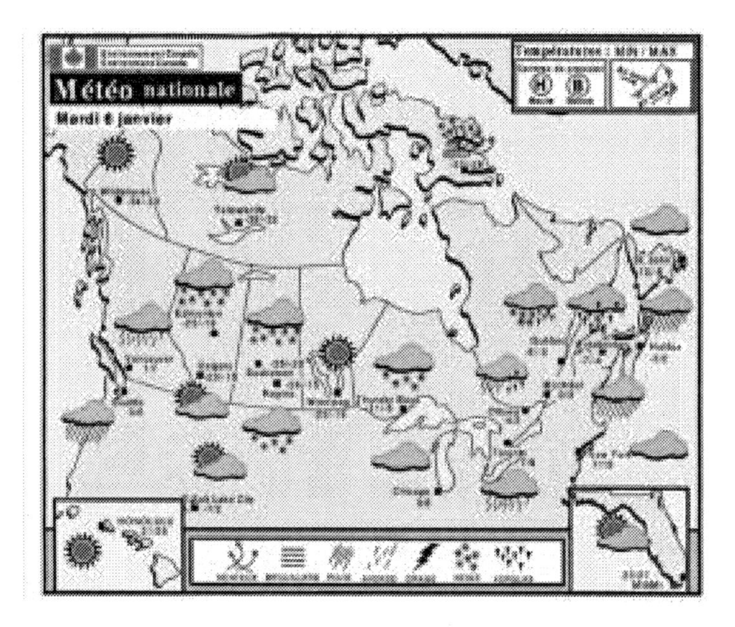

Miguel's home page

A printout of the home page of a Spanish youngster such as the one in the screen shot offers an example of some very accessible language from an authentic context and a way into producing similar text and picture presentations, whether as electronic documents on the Web or simple displays.

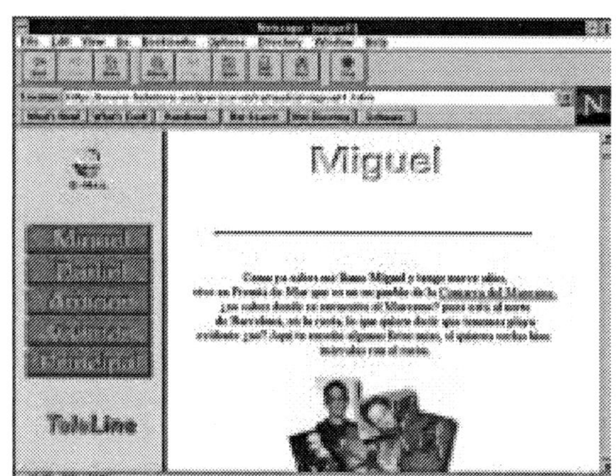

German magazine

The screen shot below shows the articles available from *Jetzt On-line.*[10] These could be printed out and used for whole class reading or to form a bank of reading materials to allow individual access and choice of reading matter.

Many of these pages can be used for general interest and students will sometimes gain more by being allowed to choose what they want to read without an accompanying task. Such free reading can also be supported through tasks such as looking up and recording any unfamiliar language and/or by producing a brief summary or report. Basic comprehension activities can also be used, such as question and answer, multiple choice, true or false, classification, sorting and matching. There is a wealth of valuable practice activities that can be devised using the exercises found in coursebooks, tests and examinations as well as more creative and open-ended tasks.

10 http://www.goethe.de/z/jetzt

Ideas for activities using printed out pages include:

- matching pictures to text;
- comprehension;
- information gap;
- creating a TV or radio news broadcast with news, sport, weather;
- writing to the author of the home page;
- using the original as a model for pupils to produce their own writing: fanzine home page, personal home page;
- reading for pleasure; on-line libraries are one possible development and a modern languages specific on-line library has been piloted as part of the Schools On-line project[11].

Tasks can be closed or open and there is good scope for differentiation, especially if a range of Web pages are available or are included with authentic materials from other sources. The whole class may work on the same printout, or each individual or group may have a different page. Jig-saw tasks in which each pupil has a different source of information to help with the completion of the final task can be very effective in encouraging co-operation within a group.

Here are some suggestions for activities to be used with different Web sites:

news stories (especially current ones already familiar to learners through press and TV)	produce a news report for radio or television news
pop star pages	an imaginary interview with the star
sports (results, reports, sites dedicated to teams, players, events)	headlines – one-line summaries of each match or event
weather	weather forecast to be given orally, preferably using a weather map *à la* Michael Fish
tourist information	write a postcard to a friend describing an imaginary visit to some of the places mentioned on the site
travel information (trains, planes)	use time-tables for information gap exercises and role plays
home pages (individual or group)	write a message for the guest book
job adverts	write a letter of application
entertainment (cinema, TV/radio listings)	produce a trailer for the film or programme

11 http://sol.ultralab.anglia.ac.uk/pages/schoolsonline/languages/mflhome.html

USING WEB PAGES ON COMPUTER

A range of activities can be developed as confidence and competence in using the Web is developed. On-line access may be needed for some activities, but many can be used effectively off-line with pages that have been downloaded and saved on a local disk or network.

Browsing the site

Pupils explore the page(s), skim reading, looking at any pictures or titles and following internal links. The purpose is to familiarise themselves with the layout of the site, the content and the context. This can be followed up by oral work in various groupings – pair, group or whole class.

¿De qué trata este site?
¿Qué has visto en el site?
¿Qué imágenes hay?
¿Qué (no) te gusta en el site?

A comprehension activity

A worksheet, based on the site, can be completed with questions to be answered, gap-filling, find the French/German, etc for, true or false, multiple choice questions, open-ended questions — opinions/impressions.

Listening

Activities can be made into aural tasks in which pupils are given a tape with various questions and tasks to be solved from the Web page. For example, students are working in a tourist office and have a tape of answer phone requests for information that can be found on the Web — admission times and prices, hotels, transport.

A grammatical task

Focus on a grammatical or linguistic point: find examples of a given tense or part of speech, collect new vocabulary, look up new words in a dictionary, develop language skills in the area of IT by learning the foreign language terms (where different from English!).

Following instructions

Because using a computer involves physical activity, pupils can be given instructions to carry out. These might involve using the mouse to click on links or menus and are a good way of familiarising students with the software and foreign language computer terms if a target language browser is used.

An information gathering exercise

This is an excellent form of activity that can incorporate research and some final task in which the students have to use the language for a real purpose. A range of skills will be covered, including reading for a purpose, understanding, grammatical skills, writing and /or speaking. Information may be gathered on a range of topics such as:

- a person;
- a place;
- a film;
- an event;

for use in a writing task, e.g. producing a poster or a brochure, or in a speaking task, e.g. an oral presentation, or guessing game, or 'A' level oral topic work.

Cybertrails

Cybertrails are a form of electronic treasure hunt in which the students follow a series of links from site to site, solving clues in order to find the next site. They work best when the computers are on-line because they depend upon following links. Following a cybertrail is a relatively safe use of on-line time as it is a very well focussed task with a clear structure so there is less chance of students browsing aimlessly. It does depend upon a fast connection, especially if used as an activity for a class involving lots of computers.

Cybertrails are available at a number of sites but very quickly become out of date unless well thought out and well maintained. Some sites offer a number of cybertrails, e.g.:

http://www.ualberta.ca/~fmillar/gymnase.html

Usually, each trail contains links to a number of other sites and the clue to be solved gives the correct link to follow. To reward the winner or all those

completing the task, there are a number of virtual prizes on the Web, e.g. a virtual trip to an exotic location or simply to a favourite (foreign language) site. Alternatively, send the successful students a virtual bouquet[12] of flowers!

Pupil generated trails might be a good way of extending the activity, especially if the pupils can use on-line time out of lessons to make them up.

Using data from Web pages in other IT applications

One of the best ways in which to exploit the Web is to save information from the Web to be used in other IT applications. This can be done with text, graphics, sound, video or a combination thereof. Teachers can produce their own original IT materials in this way, such as texts with or without graphics, and, possibly, for use in text manipulation software such as Camsoft's *Fun with Texts*. Students can also complete tasks in which they gather information from the Web in electronic form in order to produce their own reports in electronic form, for example:

- what the French/German/Spanish papers say – a collection of the main headlines from national (e.g. Belgium or Mexico) and/or regional (e.g. Bavaria or Provence) newspapers;
- a tourist brochure including one or two images;
- a poster.

Word processing

The text from a Web page can be copied and pasted into a word processing package. This is a relatively easy task which can be done in a number of ways according to the software used and, if necessary, advice should be sought from local IT support staff. Here is a step by step procedure for copying text on a PC computer:

1. Position the mouse pointer at the start of the text.
2. Hold down the left mouse button and drag down the page until all the text is highlighted.

12 http://www.cyberstation.fr/~postulka/ — I found this one using a simple search on Yahoo France. It may no longer be operational but you should be able to find others if you search again.

3. Release the mouse button.
4. Click on the EDIT menu and then on COPY.
5. The text is now copied into the SCRAPBOOK or CLIPBOARD.
6. Switch to the Word Processor (you may have to close your Web browser first depending upon the capabilities of your system).
7. Click on the EDIT menu and then on PASTE.

Such texts can be put to many different uses[13].

Text manipulation software — authoring packages

There are a number of such packages which allow you to create a text that can be used by pupils for gap-filling, line re-ordering, anagrams and other text re-construction activities. Depending upon the program, there is usually a system for scoring and supporting the learner by suggesting answers if they get stuck. Perhaps the most widely used such package is Camsoft's *Fun With Texts*.

For most authoring packages it is possible to use text from a Web page. Web pages can be saved as plain text and may then be used in the text manipulation software, although there might be some further complication to ensure success. As an example, I have set out the procedure I follow to do this in my own department where we have *Fun With Texts* and use *Netscape* as our Web browser on our PC computers.

1. Open your Web browser and find the Web page that you are going to copy text from.[14]
2. Position the mouse pointer at the start of the text.
3. Hold down the left mouse button and drag down the page until all the text is highlighted.
4. Release the mouse button.
5. Click on the EDIT menu and then on COPY.
6. The text is now copied into the SCRAPBOOK or CLIPBOARD.
7. Leave the browser and open a word processor, eg Word for Windows or Wordpad.
8. Click on the EDIT menu and then on PASTE.

13 See, for example, the ideas on pp31–32 of Atkinson T, *Co-ordinating IT in the modern languages faculty* (Rugby: ALL, 1995).

14 Be careful not to infringe copyright.

9. Save the text with a file name of maximum eight letters and the extension FWT, e.g. FILENAME.FWT. Save the file in the format MSDOS text — this will preserve the accents. Make sure that you save the file in your normal *Fun With Texts* directory.
10. Leave the word processor and start *Fun With Texts.*
11. Open the file and edit it so that the lines are the correct length.
12. Save the file and test it with one of the activities.

Short texts work well with such packages or a longer text can be divided into two or more parts. Texts must link in to language learning aims and objectives and use the appropriate vocabulary and constructions. This may mean some adaptation of the original. Some recommended text types:

- news reports;
- sports reports;
- film or record reviews;
- descriptions of places — towns, cities, regions, monuments.

Multi-media

The Web offers an excellent source of resources in various media — sound clips, images, video clips and text — on a vast range of topics. Thus it provides a ready made toolkit for students to generate multi-media projects. Collecting the information for a topic is reading with a purpose. Producing the package will involve using and editing language and the final product will be read by other students.

This kind of work is a high level IT activity in which teachers may need to plan work with the IT co-ordinator.

There are various software packages that can be used for multi-media work and it is important to select the one that pupils can use and experience across the curriculum. In this way languages can capitalise on the school's expertise and experience and build on the skills that pupils already have.

Pupils may also use the resources from the Web to help in producing their own Web pages. The Web itself is an excellent medium for publishing multi-media electronic documents and there are a number of ways of producing Web pages as described in Chapter 4.

Learning on the Net

Some sites are set up with learning activities that learners do on-line. Typically, multiple-choice activities are used. The student answers the questions and receives feedback from the remote computer. Some experimental sites offer this type of activity and a little browsing on the Net should enable you to find some currently active sites with learning activities. Such interactive sites can only be used on-line.

Individual tuition over the Net is a growth area, especially in North America where virtual schools and colleges are competing with bricks and mortar establishments. Typically, a virtual languages school offers Web based course materials and activities. The student completes the learning tasks and sends their work (written, aural, multiple choice) electronically to their tutor via the Internet and receives feedback in the same way. Look out also for managed on-line projects which involve students from different schools or countries in working collaboratively across the Net.

Some suggested activities

A reading file

Reading for pleasure can play a valuable part in language learning and offers scope for differentiation, extension, choice and flexibility. The Internet offers a wide choice of reading matter that can be printed out and used to form a classified reading scheme.

Using a colour printer (cost around £200), high quality printouts of Internet pages can be made on a wide range of topics of interest for children in a particular year group, eg hobbies, pets, school, sport, pop music, fashion, home pages of young people, environmental issues, news reports, places of interest.

The printouts can then be classified according to degree of difficulty of the language. Three categories might be used and for this it is important to obtain a range of materials within each category. A system of colour coding can be used to indicate the level of each printout. The printouts can be stored in loose-leaf folders, protected in plastic envelopes and made available to be used in lessons in various ways:

- as a filler for pupils who have finished early;
- as an optional activity in some lessons;
- as part of a carousel of activities.

The collection of printouts is ongoing and a number of folders can be accumulated so that these folders can be rotated between teachers to ensure that there is always new material available. Students soon get used to using this system and develop good reading skills including:

- the ability to select reading materials according to a combination of degree of difficulty and degree of interest in the topic;
- dictionary skills;
- recording and reviewing the printouts they have read;
- re-using the language acquired in other contexts, for example in the pupils' own writing.

The idea is not new and was first developed using conventional authentic materials — magazines, comics, newspapers and brochures. However, the Internet provides a richer and more up-to-date source of material. Particular features include:

- pupils look forward to updated printouts from sites they have read previously;
- pupils are motivated to visit sites on-line.

Research for oral topic at 'A' level and Higher Still

At this level teachers often encourage students to work independently and autonomously. If there is less emphasis on taught sessions and more on independent study, the use of the Internet is easily incorporated into the students' learning style. A set of Internet stations is needed in a readily accessible resources area such as the school library. A booking system is useful as is technical help to support students and to provide unobtrusive supervision to avoid misuse. Students can also be asked to sign a contract specifying that Internet access is for authorised study purposes only!

The modern languages department can develop a simple guide to using the Internet explaining the techniques and procedures to access the World Wide Web and providing information on recommended sites and how to search for sites in the various languages of study.

It is worth developing a system for collecting interesting sites and storing these on the computer so that students and teachers can recommend a site, perhaps with a very brief site description in the target language which can be produced by using language from the site itself. These sites should be checked and included in the list of interesting sites for each language — either in printed form or directly available on the computers, thereby avoiding re-typing of complex URLs.

Students can develop their Web skills during the 'A' level or Higher Still course at the same time as enhancing their language skills. In lessons, there can be regular opportunities for oral presentations based on a visit to a Web site. Finally, students might use the Web to research for the oral topics.

News from the Web

The latest news from the Web can be displayed on a notice board in the languages area with printouts of a range of items:

- news stories from abroad including foreign coverage of home news;
- sports updates on events abroad Tour de France, European football, Olympics;
- general interest — hedgehogs, Greenpeace, local festivals;
- home page of the week.

Naturally, it takes a lot of work to keep this up to date so the load needs to be shared between languages teachers, FLAs, student teachers and pupils, allocating responsibility for different languages and different topics.

Italian train journey

FS, the Italian state railway, has an easy to use Web site for planning a train journey which acts as an interactive time-table that can be used in a role-play simulation. When typing in the details of a journey plan, the computer will respond with the best fit, including any connections to be made. One student takes the part of the passenger and the other of the train information clerk. The dialogue might go like this:

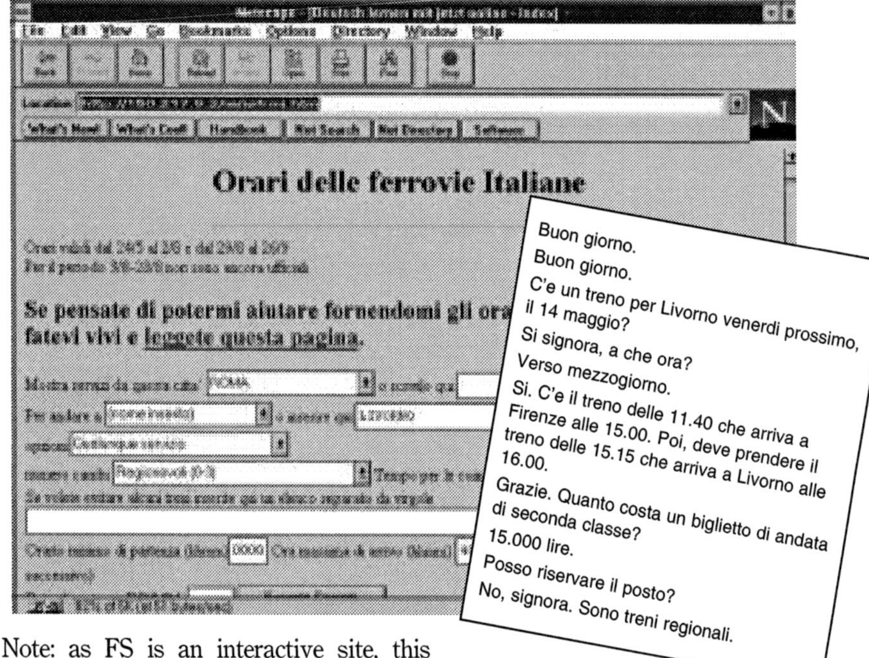

Note: as FS is an interactive site, this activity can only be used on-line. You cannot download the time-table but only interrogate it. You could produce printouts of time-table queries to use in information gaps off-line or as practice before students go on-line. In the screen shot, a query is in progress for a train from Rome to Livorno and the current query is asking for options like first class, seat reservation, cycle transport, etc.

Summary

The Web can be used in a variety of ways – printouts, on-line, off-line and in a range of IT applications. There is scope to practise all four skills and to devise activities for each stage of the learning process, from presentation and practice to genuinely communicative use of language. The range of material available is truly vast so it is possible to develop activities suited to any level and in a wide range of languages.

4 Web publishing

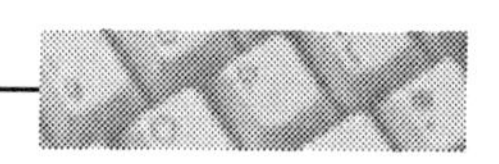

Publishing over the Web offers some exciting possibilities for using this new and rapidly expanding medium. Many schools and colleges are developing their own Web sites, using readily available tools in terms of both hardware and software as Information and Communications Technology (ICT) becomes much more accessible.

So how can schools and colleges use their Web sites to support the teaching and learning of modern languages?

To provide information

Information can be displayed on the Web about the opportunities for language learning — language choice, exchanges and trips, courses, exams, study skills. This information could be for both existing and prospective students and their parents. Initially, it might be used mainly within the school and there will be a need to decide what information is accessible publicly and what is for restricted internal access on the school's intranet (internal Internet).

To make resources available

A good starting point is to build up modern languages Web pages which provide links to Web sites of interest and guidance to students on browsing the Web, finding foreign languages sites and using the Web in languages learning.

Next, the school may be able to generate language learning activities on the Web. These can be home-made or downloaded or adapted from other Web sites

(copyright will probably only be an issue if profit is to be made). Even more simple is to point learners at activities on other Web sites. Ultimately, the Web provides a way of making many resources available to students. Possibilities include:

- texts to be read;
- worksheets;
- audio materials;
- video;
- reference lists to search for information across the world wide Web;
- course information;
- information about examinations.

In fact, there is very little that can't be put onto the Web. In the not too distant future it may become a means for delivering courseware, although it is likely that commercial publishers will undertake this rather than individuals or departments. In universities, where the Web has been used for the last decade or so, there are some interesting examples of how far the process has gone. However, much of the material is only accessible from within each university so you will only be able to get a general idea of what has been done. Try a visit to your local university's Web site.

To publish students' work

As an outlet for students' creative work, the Web offers access to a global audience, including native speakers and language learners in many different countries. Students can have a meaningful audience for their work and one which may well provide feedback in the target language. The Web can provide a showcase for writing, art work, photographs, audio recordings and even video.

Learning to publish for this medium calls for a range of skills. Solid blocks of text are fairly unappealing and may go unheeded. If the aim is to get feedback, then the content has to be framed in a way that encourages and facilitates it. If a lively topic is chosen and interesting views/questions are included, it is more likely to capture the interest of the audience.

There are many school pupils who have developed their own home pages, either at school or at home. Since they are learning a foreign language and since their

page can be read by many speakers of that language, there is a good basis for adding a foreign language section. The content area will be decided by the student — hopefully nothing too horrendous. This activity might be integrated into their regular language learning work or could be tackled as an extra-curricular activity or project. The Web has great potential for encouraging language use outside of designated lesson time.

A concern will be to protect children from any kind of danger so that care must be taken in the nature of the information provided on the Web. Personal details, contact details and photographs all need to be handled in a sensitive and secure manner and this is all part of educating students to this new and powerful medium and its hidden dangers.

To provide Web-based learning opportunities

As a publishing medium the Web allows you to write and publish activities for your students. The Web is a communications medium so you can use it to communicate any task or information to your students.

The information could be made accessible from the school's internal network only or could be live on the Internet for those students with the facility to access it from home. Web pages have a number of features that make them a powerful learning medium:

- multi-media;
- hyperlinking;
- interactivity.

To market languages services

In these commercial times schools may wish to market language services via the Internet. For example, developing foreign language Web pages for local businesses or agencies.

To make contacts and work collaboratively

The Web is a good place to find link partners for actual or virtual exchanges. A virtual exchange could involve the joint production of a Web page with the link school. Schools with their own Web pages can use them to advertise for the kinds of links and exchanges that they are seeking. This process can be very specific if individual pupils have their own Web pages.

To publish teacher's home pages

What do ML teachers put on their home pages? Here are a few ideas:

- professional development — what you are working on and any professional contacts or exchanges you might be seeking, e.g. assessment for a specific coursebook, developing materials for an 'A' level topic;
- consultancy offered in languages services or professional development;
- contact details, especially e-mail;
- interests: some people develop Web sites based on these;
- a virtual languages school.

How to write pages for the Web

The creation of Web pages may seem a daunting task and a simple audit of your own IT skills should tell you if you can take this on.

1. Are you a complete IT novice? If so, this may be beyond your immediate capabilities. You might do better to develop a reasonable competence in word processing and/or desktop publishing before attempting to make Web pages.
2. Are you competent in using a computer for word processing and can you manage these basic operations:
   - operating a mouse to click on menus, etc;
   - saving files to disk and organising your files in folders or directories;
   - page layout;
   - adding graphics to a document, e.g. clip art.

If so and you are willing to learn by doing, you should be able to produce a basic Web page in a couple of hours.

There are various ways of producing Web pages. An easy starting point is to check if your word processing package or desktop publishing package has a Web page option — from 1997 on most new packages have this facility. If so, you lay out your page as you want it to appear on the screen. The completed file can then be viewed with a browser to check that it is as you want it. This method is very simple but limits you to those facilities provided by your package. It also means that you may produce quite large files that may be slow to load and difficult to update or edit. These disadvantages may be overcome by new software releases.

Already, MicrosoftWord 7 and Netscape Communicator offer very good Web authoring facilities. If you have access to programs such as these, you will be well advised to try your hand at producing a Web page following their tutorials and help pages.

Another way to produce Web pages is to learn to use the Web page language – hypertext mark-up language (HTML). The computer shops have a range of manuals to help you do this. Browsing through these should soon help you to choose one that is relatively jargon free. One that I found useful is:

Lemay L, *Teach yourself Web publishing with HTML 3.2 in a week* (Indianapolis: Samsnet, 1996) — look out for more recent editions.

The basics of writing for the Web

Here is a very brief step by step guide to producing a Web page using hypertext mark-up language (HTML).

To do this you need a simple word processing package such as:

- Notepad (available on all PCs in the accessories group);
- Wordpad — provided with Windows 95;

or any word processing package that allows you to create plain text files, e.g. Microsoft Word .

A simple Web page is displayed on the next page and the HTML code for the page is shown below it.

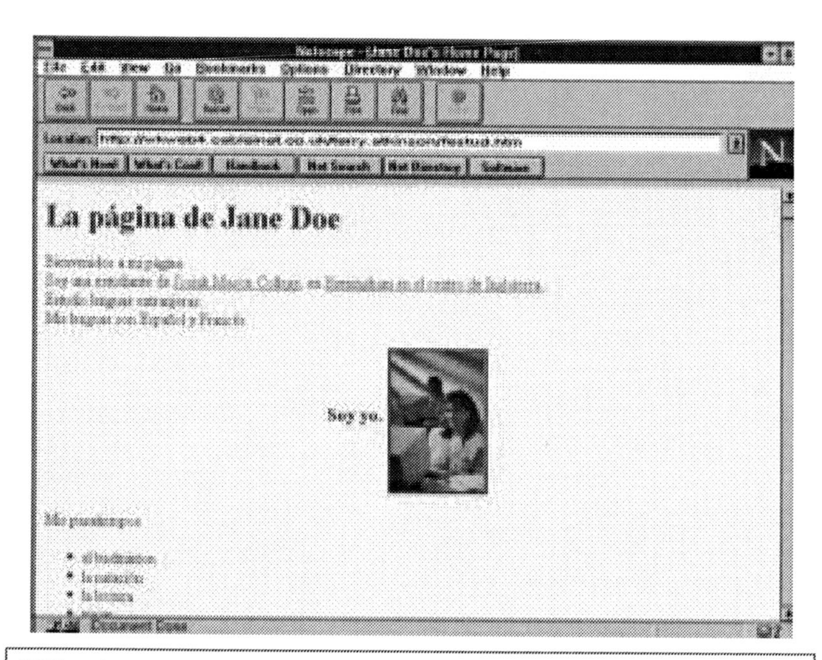

HTML code

```
<htm>
<body bgcolor="#FFEBCD" text="#008000" link="#FF00FF" v-link="#800030">
<title>Jane Doe's Home Page</title>
<h1>La página de Jane Doe</h1>
<p>Bienvenidos a mi página<br>
Soy una estudiante de <a href="http://www.rmplc.co.uk/eduWeb/sites/canavan/index.html">Josiah
Mason College</a>, en <a href="http://www.birmingham.co.uk/">Birmingham en el centro de
Inglaterra.</a>.<br>
Estudio lenguas extranjeras.<br>
Mis lenguas son Español y Francés.</p>
<h3 align=center>Soy yo. <img align=middle src="jane.jpg"border=3></h3>
<p>Mis pasatiempos</p>
<ul>
<li>el badminton</li>
<li/>la natación</li>
<li>la lectura</li>
<li>viajar</li>
</ul>
¿Te gustaría ver algo de mi trabajo?? <a href=
"http://www.rmplc.co.uk/eduWeb/sites/canavan/mlstudent.html">
<img align=middle src=click.jpg></a>
<p>Si te gustaría escribirme, por favor aprovechar mi e-mail para ponernos en contacto:<a
href="mailto:jane.doe@josiah.mason.ac.uk.">jane.doe@josiah.mason.ac.uk</a></p>
</body>
</htm>
```

Step 1

Type in the HTML code as shown above on your word processor or text editor (e.g. Notepad) and save it as plain text with a file name with HTM as the extension, e.g.: page.htm

Step 2

View *page.htm* by opening the file with your browser (Netscape or Internet Explorer).

Step 3

Your page should look like the Web page on p42. If not, check that the code is exactly as given above and correct any errors, save the corrected code as *page.htm* and open the file anew in the browser.

Step 4

To make changes to the page and to make your own original pages you need to understand the tags and the syntax governing their use. Tags are discussed in some detail below. All tags are enclosed in angled brackets thus: <tag>

Anything not enclosed thus will appear on the Web page, i.e. your text. Apart from the exceptions below, tags must be opened and closed thus:

opening tags	**closing tags**
<title>	</title>
<body>	</body>
<h1>	</h1>

The exceptions are tags which do not require closing:

 inserts a line break <HR> inserts a line on screen

Some tags need qualifiers to work and these qualifiers are enclosed in speech marks. Examples are:

links to other Web pages:
<A HREF="http://www.leeds.ac.uk/">The University of Leeds</A>

images to be displayed on the page:
<IMG SRC="picture.jpg"></IMG>

Colours

You need to choose colours for (a) background (**bgcolor**); (b) **text** ; (c) **link** ; and (d) **v-link**, which is the colour a piece of linked text changes to after it has been visited. If you do not specify what colours you want , by default the background is usually white, text black, links blue and v-links red.

In order for your page to be easily read, choose either a very pale background and very dark text, or vice versa.

It is possible to specify many shades of colour, but not all browsers will support them, and they may turn out looking quite different to what you intended; therefore it makes sense to stick to some basic colours which I have listed below.

Black	White	Blue
#000000	#FFFFFF	#0000FF
Red	**Green**	**Cream**
#FF0000	#008000	#FFEBCD
Silver	**Magenta**	**Purple**
#C0C0C0	#FF00FF	#800030

Tags

Tags are the bits of HTML which you put around your text and images in order to make them appear as you want them on the screen. Remember: **you cannot alter the way your page looks on the screen by the way you arrange text and images on your HTML page — you can only do this by using tags.**

These are some of the most basic tags:

<htm>.....</htm>	goes round all of your HTML page
<body>....</body>	encases all you have written. It is also the tag within which you specify your colour choices if you wish.
<title>...</title>	this is what someone searching the Net will see — make it short and sensible!
<h> ...</h>	encloses a heading. You can make the text of your heading bigger or smaller by giving <h> a number — <h1> is the largest heading and <h6> is the smallest.
<p>...</p>	encloses a paragraph.
<img src>	denotes that you are going to insert an image — **src** means source,so you have to define the filename of your image, e.g.**<img src="jane.jpg">** Images can be inserted within headings or paragraphs.
** **	means new line. Use this if you want to make your text start a new line within a heading or paragraph.
<a href>....</a>	makes a link, and goes around the piece of text or image that you want to link.
mailto: goes inside **<a href>…</a>**	makes a link directly to an e-mail address.
<ul>…</ul>	encloses a list; **<li>**goes inside **<ul>…</ul>**and comes before each item on the list.

You will see that the general rule is: **if you *open* a tag, you must remember to *close* it again.**

If you are having problems getting your page to work, the first thing to do is to go through your HTML page making sure you have closed all your tags.

Publishing your page

You can view your page on the Web by opening it as a file as in step 2. This is useful to look at changes as you are developing the page. To publish the page on the Web enables others to see your page and to do this you need to upload — this means transferring your file to a computer that acts as an Internet server. If you are uploading to your school or college's Web site, this will usually be managed by your IT staff who will probably simply require a disk with your file on it. If you have your own Web space from an Internet provider, you will need to see their documentation on how to transfer your file to their server. This will

involve using FTP software which is freely available on the Internet from sites such as Tucows.[15] Once installed, the FTP program enables you to log on to the server and move files between your computer and the server .

Publishing on the Net for teachers and learners — Case studies

School A

At this school, a Year 9 class undertook a project to produce Web pages in German describing their school which were then published as part of the school's Web site. This was largely an information providing activity.

The project was undertaken collectively with different students responsible for the content of different pages which were then linked together to form the German section of the school's site. The pupils used the school's digital camera to photograph the school so that the pages are illustrated.

This was a useful collaborative project which helped raise the profile of the department and of the school. The key question is, why do this? It does encourage a range of learning and leads to an attractive end product which might be useful to the link school. If a school exchange is a regular occurrence, the site could be tailored to the needs of the visitors and updated or re-designed each time the exchange happens.

English language business services

This was a pilot project devised by a TEFL teacher to provide on-line personal tuition. There are two main services offered. The correction and improvement of business documents is a business service with a language element. Subscribers can select some or all of the following areas for checking and correction:

- language errors — grammar, lexis, spelling;
- register;
- style.

Personal tuition is also available in a range of settings of use to business people.

15 http://www.idiscover.co.uk/tucows/

The service provides learning tasks to be completed by learners and sent electronically to tutors for correction and feedback. It also makes available the facility for real time interaction between tutor and learner using Internet Relay Chat (IRC) — a written dialogue which has the advantage of much lower cost than an international phone call.

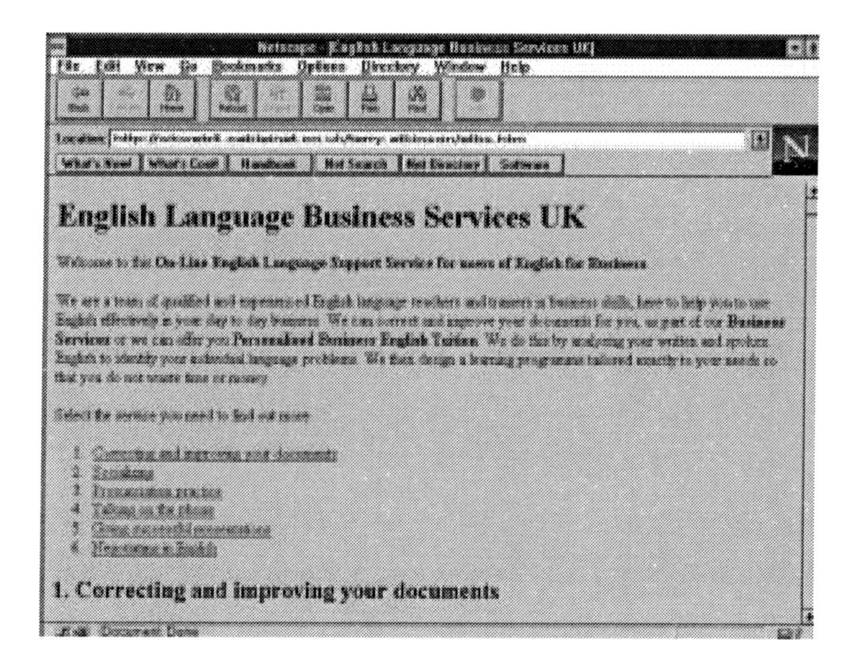

Schools B & C

Two secondary schools decided to explore publishing students' work on the Internet in order to see if writing for the Web provided a good learning opportunity and if feedback from those reading it could be received and further encourage learning.

In School B, the pages were produced in French initially, although subsequently Spanish pages were also added. The work was tackled as an extension activity by high achieving pupils in Year 9. The topic chosen was school and the teacher used material from various sources to teach the topic, e.g. Studio 16. The final task was for individuals to produce pages giving their opinions on their own school which, it was hoped, would inspire replies from native speakers or other learners of the target language. The pages were published with an invitation to send feedback to a collective e-mail managed by the modern languages staff. The pages included photographs taken with the school's digital camera.

At School C a similar approach was taken but here Year 10 students worked in pairs to produce a page with a photograph of each and information about themselves — family, pets, likes and dislikes. Again, an e-mail contact address was given which was common to all students and managed by staff. From these two projects it was clear that both staff and students found the idea motivating, perhaps because of its novelty. It is, at the very least, an interesting variation on the use of display. The two key considerations are to get effective feedback and to avoid or filter out anything undesirable. With hindsight, feedback will only be forthcoming if the pages are written with this in mind. Actually finding an audience is not so easy. The pages were advertised but little feedback came. In future, targeting an audience will be tried — a class in another school in the target language country or simply another class learning the target language. This should lead to guaranteed and appropriate feedback and avoid any undesirable responses. At School A the activity is now being incorporated into schemes of work where it will probably be used as extension.

Berlin project

This an activity for lower sixth formers in which they must plan a visit to Berlin on a given budget. Activities include booking accommodation and travel and planning excursions. All the tasks are set out on a Web page authored by the teacher and encoded with the help of students. The page also contains all the links needed by the students.

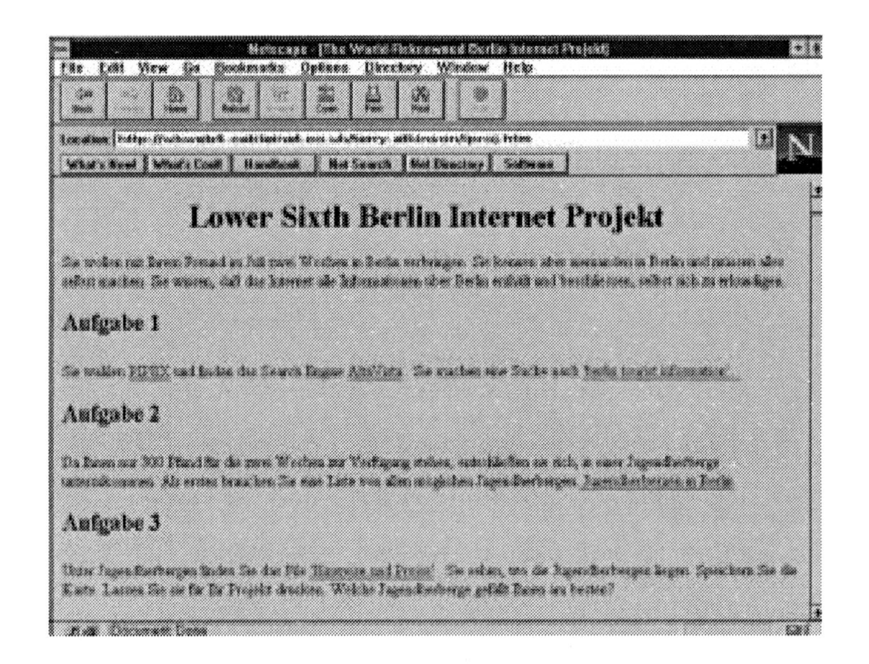

GETTING STARTED WITH USING THE WEB FOR LEARNING MATERIALS

The facility to use hyperlinks can be exploited in a number of ways to support language learning:

Context sensitive help

Use a text that you have written yourself or copied or adapted from elsewhere. The Web itself is the most obvious source and has the advantage that the text is already in HTML form. Next, decide which words or phrases may cause difficulty to students. These words are made into hyperlinks that take the user to the appropriate point in a help file. The help given will depend upon the students, but possibilities include pictures, translations, synonyms, target language definitions, cognates.

Question and answer

Self-correcting exercises can be provided via hyperlinks. The question is linked to the answer so that students can click to find out if they are right or simply to find the answer if they don't know it. Computer marking is possible but would require the skills of a programmer and is, in any case, of questionable benefit.

Picture choice

Two or more pictures are provided along with a question which could be in written or oral form. The students answer the question by clicking on the appropriate picture and then receive feedback as to whether or not they have answered correctly.

Once started on the production of such materials, the possibilities will tend to grow. The sharing of the materials via the Internet is a probable development and one that is envisaged as a key part of the National Grid for Learning.

Summary

Publishing on the Web has many exciting possibilities but does depend upon a degree of technical competence that many languages teachers may not have the time to develop. This may not be a problem if the school can provide technical support, so it is important for teachers to realise what they could achieve with such support, for example the opportunity to publish students' work and to create Web-based learning materials. School Web sites are growing rapidly and there is plenty of scope for modern languages pages to be prominent.

5 Managing the Net

The Web is a complex and powerful resource which needs careful managing to ensure efficient and appropriate use. Policies need to be decided at a whole school level with regard to on-line access, and it is important that languages departments contribute to policy formation, especially as there is such great potential on the Web for language learning, arguably more than in other subjects.

Managing Web resources

Printing a Web page

To print out a Web page including text and any images, use the file menu as shown here while on-line (Netscape 3):

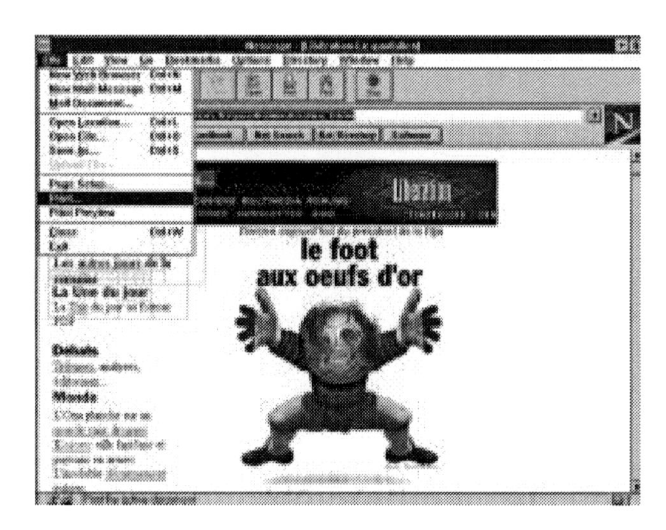

This will allow Web pages to be used in the classroom. Printouts can be quite effective in black and white, but colour is better. Some sites run over several pages and can be difficult to print out effectively. It is also possible to print out the images on Web pages, but they must first be saved to disk – see below.

Saving a Web page (text only)

To save a Web page, use the file menu as in this example from Internet Explorer 4:

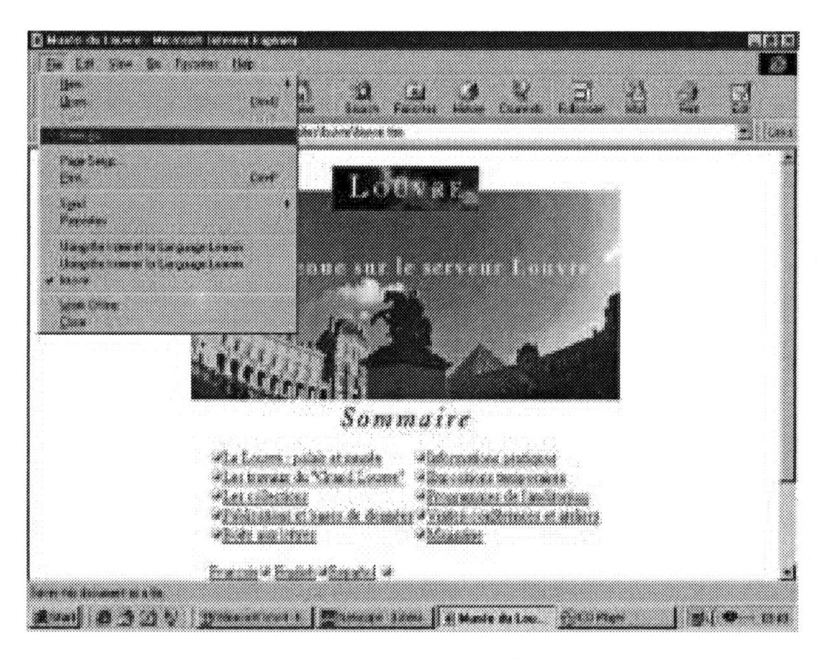

This method will save the text only. You can reload the file using your Web browser but the text only will be displayed. Any images will not be shown.

Copying an image from a Web page

To copy an image, click on the image using the right hand mouse button. This will bring up a menu, as shown in the screen shot below, from which you can save the image.

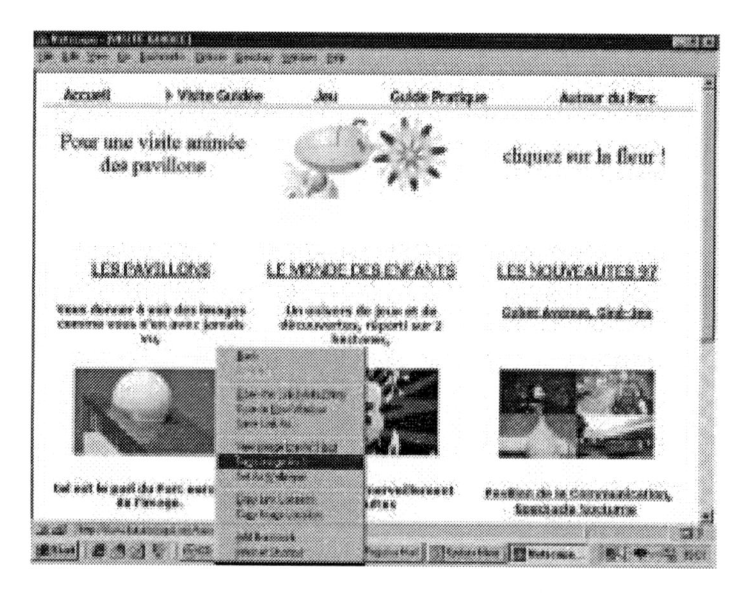

You can then import the image into other applications such as word processing software or desktop publishing, provided they can accept the image format, usually GIF or JPG.

Copying some text

The easiest way to copy text from a Web page is to highlight the text using the mouse. You can then paste the text into a word processor. This is the best way to generate new files for *Fun With Texts.*

Saving a Web page (text and images)

This can be complex and it may be best to seek help from an IT specialist if this is available. Your Internet browser will have a save facility which you can access from the file menu. However, this will probably save the text only. To save the images you will have to follow the procedure given on p52 for copying images. It should now be possible to view both text and images by opening the saved version of the page from your hard disk or floppy. However, if the images are still not visible, technical assistance will be needed to ensure that the images are in the appropriate directory.

Copying a Web site

This requires special software tools which can be bought from computer shops or downloaded over the Web from FTP sites such as Tucows.[16]

Making Web pages available off-line

Many schools are beginning to download Web pages in order to make these available via the school's computers. This avoids the need for students to go on-line but, as the previous paragraphs demonstrate, it does call for some technical expertise. Copyright will have to be considered and permission to download a page or pages can be sought.

Some simple Web page authoring will be required to enable students to access the downloaded pages. This would entail a page giving brief information about each site and a link to access it via the school's network or hard disk or floppy — yes, you can save Web pages on a floppy disk.

ACCESS

Access to computer facilities in languages departments has always been patchy and the Internet demands additional equipment that may only gradually become available. If, as in some schools, there is only one computer connected to the Internet and that is located in the staffroom or some other area off limits to students, it will be impossible to use the Internet on-line. However, off-line use may be a better way forward and will greatly limit the telephone costs.

INTRANET

Many schools are developing their own Intranets, which are effectively miniature Internets with selected Web sites. An Intranet functions in the same way as the Internet but operates across the school's network so that the Web pages are readily accessible by any networked computers without the need for a modem or phone line. It is even possible to save the Intranet pages on floppy disks for use on computers that are not connected to the network.

16 http://www.idiscover.co.uk/tucows/

Typically the Intranet will have its pages organised by department or faculty. Clicking on the MFL section takes you into the departmental home page. From here you can access the pages created by the department or ones that have been downloaded from the Internet.

Intranet limitations

Downloading pages from the Internet may be technically possible but can be quite tricky. However, copyright issues also need to be considered. The current position is very unclear. To be certain, permission should be obtained from the copyright holder but in practice the copyright holder will not be able to respond to all such requests. Limited copying for educational purposes may well be acceptable but any commercial use of material may not.

A second limitation of the Intranet is that many hyperlinks will not work, reducing the flexibility of the medium. Thus, surfing is limited to the pages of the Intranet.

Learning materials on the Intranet

If the department creates its own Web based learning materials these will form a key part of the Intranet. In fact HTML, the language used for writing Web pages, is a good medium for writing learning materials and this has been used extensively by some university teachers who have had access to the medium for some time.

Benefits of using intranets

- Speed of access — dependent on your server alone.
- Greater reliability — from bitter experience it can ruin a carefully prepared session if the on-line Internet connection slows to a near standstill or gives up entirely. A trial of your activity on your own may work fine, but when fifteen computers in the lab all request the same page at the same time you can hit problems!!!

MANAGING INNOVATION WITH TECHNOLOGY

The possibilities of new technology are both exciting and frightening, so it is important to consider the factors which are likely to lead to its successful

adoption. The items in the table below are based on classroom experience and on the lessons learned from a range of initiatives such as the MFLIT[17] and Schools On-line[18] projects.

+ positive factors	− negative factors
■ partnership between IT co-ordinator and MFL teachers	■ lack of time
■ support of senior management	■ lack of access
■ focus on learning outcomes	■ lack of training
■ integration of IT work into schemes of work	■ lack of support from advisory staff
■ access to advisory staff in MFL and IT	■ technical problems (Pam Haezewindt distinguishes between initial technical difficulties and persistent technical difficulties)
■ access to training	■ poor siting of hardware
■ ease of access to hardware	■ lack of support from IT co-ordinator who, however willing, may not have time or expertise
■ collaborative approach by MFL teachers	■ lack of basic IT skills in MFL dept
	■ working in isolation

TRAINING

The Internet is a new medium so that there are new skills to be acquired. For those who lack confidence in using computers, this will be daunting unless time and effort is given over to training. The aim of training must be to achieve a basic competence so that teachers will have the confidence to tackle using the Internet with a class. Of course, there will always be those students who know all there is to know about the Net and their expertise can be acknowledged and harnessed, but only if the teacher has enough understanding to follow what is happening.

Training is best provided in-house with the MFL teachers working together with the IT co-ordinator to learn how to use the hardware and software that the school actually has. Externally provided INSET is a useful addition, especially if it is focused clearly on MFL.

17 http://vtc.ngfl.gov.uk/resource/cits/mfl

18 http://sol.ultralab.anglia.ac.uk/pages/schoolsonline/languages/mflhome.html

In planning a training programme with the IT co-ordinator it will be helpful to decide on the core skills. These will probably include:

- making the Internet connection — usually through an automated dial-up;
- starting up the Internet software;
- accessing a page for which the URL is known;
- navigating the Web;
- closing down.

Extension skills might include:

- searching the Web;
- book marking favourite sites;
- printing;
- copying text or images;
- saving Web pages;
- using text and images from the Web in a word processor or desktop publishing package, etc.

Summary

The use of the Internet in language learning brings with it a new set of challenges for the organisational and managerial capacities of modern languages departments. While some of these issues are likely to be decided at a whole school level, it is crucial that the modern languages teachers contribute to policy formation so that the needs of the subject are taken into account.

The training of teachers in the use of this new medium should be given a priority and the process has to be seen in the context of the management of change. Some important lessons are to be learned from the early experience of pilot projects — see, for example, *Accent on IT* (1997).

6 Glossary and references

WWW Glossary

English	Definition
bookmark/favourite site	bookmarks are used to mark a favourite Web site or Web page so that it can be found again (p21)
browser	software used to display Web pages on computer
cyberspace	the internet's supposed territory
download	to transfer data (pictures, text, programs) from a remote computer to a local one
e-zine	magazine published electronically via the Internet
file transfer protocol (FTP)	software used to transfer data from a remote site to a local computer
ftp site	site which hosts libraries of downloadable software
home page	Web page for one individual or organisation
hyperlink	a link to another section of a page, to another page or to another Web site
hypertext	page system making use of links which point the user to new locations within the pages
hypertext mark-up language (HTML)	computer coding used for creating Web pages and making hyperlinks
hypertext transfer protocol (HTTP)	used to download Web pages
inter relay chat (IRC)	live discussion groups

Internet	global system for connecting computers
Intranet	local system for connecting computers
ISDN	International Standard Digital Network (fast phone line)
links	see hyperlinks
modem	device for connecting computer to telephone line for Internet, including WWW and e-mail
news group	discussion group
off-line	computer is disconnected from the Internet
on-line	computer is connected to the Internet
plug-ins	software that enhances the capacity of a browser, e.g. for audio or video
search engine	software that helps you search the World Wide Web
server	computer that hosts Web pages and/or e-mail
service providers	organisation that provides Internet services to users
site	see Web site
surfing	navigating from page to page on the internet
upload	transfer data (e.g. Web page) from local computer to remote computer (e.g. server)
ultimate/universal resource location (URL)	address of a Web page usually in a format such as: http://www.dfee.gov.uk
virtual	computer simulation, e.g. virtual trip to Berlin by visiting Berlin Web sites
Web page	a Web page is really a Web document which can have any length from a few lines to several hundred lines but which is accessed through one address
Web site	a series of interlinked Web pages such as the site of a school, college, company, local authority
World Wide Web (WWW)	global system of electronic documents accessible via the Internet

References

Atkinson T, *Co-ordinating IT in the modern languages faculty* (Rugby: ALL, 1995)

Brown E, *CALL Report 13 — Exploiting the Internet: a rich resource for language learning* (CILT, 1997)

DfEE, *National Grid for Learning* (DFEE consultation document, 1997)

Hewer S, *Text manipulation: computer-based activities to improve knowledge and use of the target language* (CILT, 1997)

Lemay L, *Teach yourself Web publishing with HTML 3.2 in a week* (Indianapolis: Samsnet, 1996) — look out for more recent editions

Little D, S Devitt and D Singleton, *Learning foreign languages from authentic texts: theory and practice* (Dublin: Authentik, 1989)

MFLIT, *Accent on IT* (NCET, 1997)

Townshend K, *E-mail: using electronic communications in foreign language teaching* (CILT, 1997)

Software

Fun With Texts, Camsoft

Internet Explorer, Microsoft

Jeu du Mai, CNDP, France

Netscape, Netscape

Websnake, Idiscover